Orangutans
Up Close

Carmen Bredeson

E Enslow Elementary

CONTENTS

WORDS TO KNOW

insects [IHN sehkts]—Bugs such as ants or flies.

pouch [POUCH]—A bag or sack.

stalk [STAWK]—A plant stem.

Parts of an Orangutan [uh RANG uh TAN]

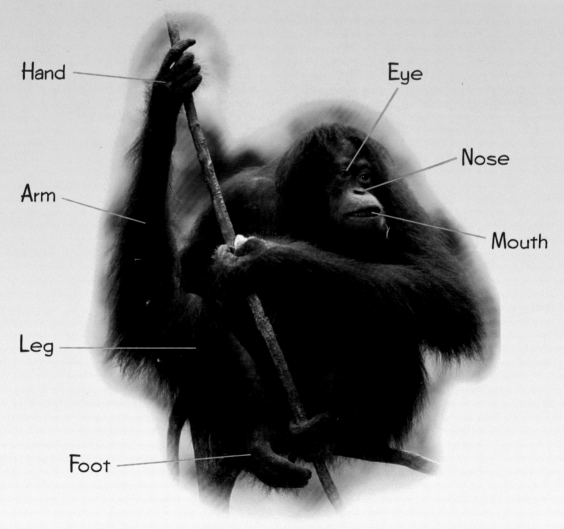

Hand

Eye

Nose

Arm

Mouth

Leg

Foot

ORANGUTAN HOMES

Orangutans live in thick forests. They spend most of their time in the trees. Males sometimes come down to the ground. Females and babies usually stay high in the trees where they are safe.

Borneo

Sumatra

Orangutans live only on these two islands.

ORANGUTAN ARMS AND LEGS

UP CLOSE

An orangutan's arms are MUCH longer than its legs. The long arms can reach very far to pick fruit. Climbing from branch to branch is easy for orangutans. Their arms and legs are very strong.

ORANGUTAN HANDS AND FEET

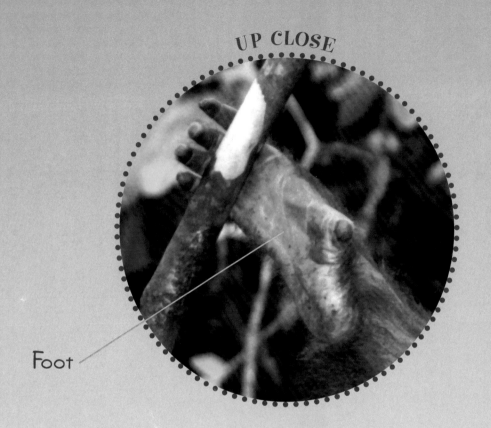

Foot

An orangutan has four fingers and a thumb on each hand. Orangutan feet have five toes each. The big toes work like extra thumbs. Orangutans can hold things with their hands or feet.

ORANGUTAN BABY

A baby orangutan stays close to its mother.
The mother teaches her baby which fruit to eat.
She shows the little orangutan how to climb.
Baby orangutans spend seven or eight years
learning from their mothers.

ORANGUTAN MOUTH

An orangutan has a big mouth and strong jaws. It can carry a whole **stalk** of bananas in its mouth. Fruit is an orangutan's favorite food. It also eats plants, nuts, small animals, and **insects**.

ORANGUTAN TOOLS

Orangutans break open fruit and nuts with rocks.
They use sticks to dig for insects in tree bark.
When it rains, orangutans get under big leaves.
They use the leaves like umbrellas.

ORANGUTAN CHEEK PADS

Male orangutans start to change when they are about fifteen years old. They grow big cheek pads. The hair on their arms grows longer. These things make the males look big and strong.

ORANGUTAN THROAT POUCH

A male orangutan has a large **pouch** under his chin. He takes a big breath of air. The pouch blows up like a balloon. Then the orangutan lets out the air. This makes a long call that can be heard for a mile.

ORANGUTAN SLEEPING NEST

Each night an orangutan finds a new place to sleep. The orangutan bends tree branches to make a soft bed. A male sleeps alone in his tree nest. A female sleeps with her babies.

20

LIFE CYCLE

A baby orangutan weighs about four pounds at birth.

A one-year-old orangutan learns to climb and play.

Females can have babies when they are about ten years old.

Adult orangutans live up to 45 years.

LEARN MORE

BOOKS

Hughes, Monica. *Orangutan Baby.* New York: Bearport Publishing Company, 2006.

Murray, Julie. *Orangutans.* Edina, Minn.: ABDO Publishing Company, 2004.

Underwood, Deborah. *Watching Orangutans in Asia.* Chicago: Heinemann Library, 2006.

WEB SITES

National Geographic Kids
<http://www.nationalgeographic.com/kids/creature_feature/0102.orangutans2.html>

San Diego Zoo
<http://www.sandiegozoo.org/animalbytes/t-orangutan.html>

INDEX

Series Literacy Consultant:
Allan A. De Fina, Ph.D.
Past President of the New Jersey Reading Association
Chairperson, Department of Literacy Education
New Jersey City University
Jersey City, New Jersey

Science Consultant:
Patrick Thomas, Ph.D.
General Curator
Bronx Zoo
Wildlife Conservation Society
Bronx, New York

Note to Parents and Teachers: The **Zoom In on Animals!** series supports the National Science Education Standards for K–4 science. The Words to Know section introduces subject-specific vocabulary words, including pronunciation and definitions. Early readers may need help with these new words.

Enslow Elementary, an imprint of Enslow Publishers, Inc.

Enslow Elementary® is a registered trademark of Enslow Publishers, Inc.

Copyright © 2009 by Carmen Bredeson

Library of Congress Cataloging-in-Publication Data

Bredeson, Carmen.
    Orangutans up close / Carmen Bredeson.
        p. cm. — (Zoom in on animals!)
    Summary: "Provides an up-close look at orangutans for new
    readers"—Provided by publisher.
    Includes bibliographical references and index.
    ISBN-13: 978-0-7660-3078-7
    ISBN-10: 0-7660-3078-4
    1. Orangutan—Juvenile literature. I. Title.
    QL737.P96B714 2009
    599.88'3—dc22   2007039466

Printed in the United States of America

10 9 8 7 6 5 4 3 2 1

To Our Readers: We have done our best to make sure all Internet Addresses in this book were active and appropriate when we went to press. However, the author and the publisher have no control over and assume no liability for the material available on those Internet sites or on other Web sites they may link to. Any comments or suggestions can be sent by e-mail to comments@enslow.com or to the address on the back cover.

✿Enslow Publishers, Inc., is committed to printing our books on recycled paper. The paper in every book contains 10% to 30% post-consumer waste (PCW). The cover board on the outside of each book contains 100% PCW. Our goal is to do our part to help young people and the environment too!

Photo Credits: © 1999, Artville, LLC, p. 4; © Anup Shah/naturepl.com, pp. 11, 15, 22 (top right); © Danita Delimont/Alamy, pp. 4(5; © Frans Lanting/Minden Pictures, p. 3; © Images&Stories/Alamy, p. 17; © iStockphoto.com/Kitch Bain, p. 10; © iStockphoto.com/pederk, pp. 1, 16; © iStockphoto.com/Timothy Dowling, p. 18; © Jean Paul Ferrero/ardea.com, p. 20; © Jonathan Hewitt/Alamy, p. 14; © 2008 Jupiterimages Corporation, p. 8; Mark Newman/Photo Researchers, Inc., p. 7; Oliver Spalt, p. 22 (top left); © Redmond Durrell/Alamy, p. 13; © Shane Moore/Animals Animals, p. 21; © Shin Yoshino/Minden Pictures, p. 6; Shutterstock, pp. 12, 22 (bottom); © Theo Allofs/Visuals Unlimited, p. 9; Thomas & Pat Leeson/Photo Researchers, Inc., p. 19.

Front Cover: © Danita Delimont/Alamy (top right); © iStockphoto.com/ Kitch Bain (bottom right); © iStockphoto.com/pederk (left); Shutterstock (center right)

Back Cover: Shutterstock

Enslow Elementary
an imprint of
Enslow Publishers, Inc.
40 Industrial Road
Box 398
Berkeley Heights, NJ 07922
USA
http://www.enslow.com